TWENTY TIPS ON PSYCHOLOGY

Titles by Herbert N. Casson
in the
Business Success Series

TWENTY TIPS ON PSYCHOLOGY

Herbert N. Casson

Tynron Press
England

© Herbert N. Casson
Tynron Press, 1995

This revised and updated edition published in 1995 by
Tynron Press
Unit 3
Turnpike Close
Lutterworth
Leicestershire LE17 4JA
U.K.

ISBN 1-85646-106-8

Cover design by Tony Chiang and Michael Wong
Typeset by Media Distribution Sdn Bhd
Printed in Singapore by General Printing Services Pte Ltd

CONTENTS

INTRODUCTION

This book is not for theoreticians – those who merely teach or study business, but for practitioners – owners and managers of business companies, large or small, whose heads are not up in the clouds and whose feet are planted firmly on the ground. Casson imparts business acumen acquired through experience and proven on the shop floor and in the market place. He uses simple, forceful words, not the pseudo-technical jargon of most modern books on business.

Where necessary, statistics and examples have been revised and updated, but the points which Herbert Casson made and the practices which he advocated need no modification. They are timeless.

No one will be able to read this book without saying, many times, "Why, that's common sense! Why didn't I think of it before!" And that is the strength of all of Herbert Casson's books. Whatever your line of business, he teaches you how to increase net profits through measures directed by sound common sense.

PREFACE

There are today thousands of books on psychology in the English language alone. The study of the science has attracted the keen interest of people in the business world. They are now recognizing its immense value in self-development and business-building.

Psychology was originally regarded as a subject only for philosophers, who developed its theories into "laws". They shrouded the whole subject in abstractions. They turned it into a metaphysical mystery, wholly incomprehensible to the average person. No one, a couple of centuries ago, would have dreamed of suggesting that psychology would one day have a practical value.

Then about 130 years ago, there came a new generation of professors of psychology. They set out, very crudely at first, to apply the principles of psychology to the everyday activities of people. They applied them to advertising, and the value of many of their suggestions was at once recognized by the most progressive advertising people. Then they applied these principles to salesmanship and to management and to the promotion of success and happiness. And several schools of thought sprang up that applied them to the preservation of mental health.

However, the psychology that was taught then was, in the main, the old-fashioned metaphysical sort that had been created by the philosophers. It was based more on theories than on facts. There was at first no data, as philosophers were not supposed to need facts.

The result was that when the psychologists set out to teach their principles outside of their universities, they learned more than they taught. They came into touch with the needs of the everyday world. They began to do research work - to gather and classify facts. And eventually this led to a re-evaluation of the study of psychology.

The literature of psychology is still a mixture of the old and the new - useless and useful - metaphysics and science. Some writers still use the old lingo that should have been done away with. Some theories have survived, although they are not sustained by facts. Because of the old metaphysical litter that still exists, a sizable proportion of practical people do not seem to be as keenly interested in psychology as they should be. They still regard it as an academic subject. The thought does not occur to business people, for instance, that it might help them to lower their costs, to sell more goods or increase the competitiveness of their business.

I have endeavored to make clear the nature of this New Psychology in this book. And I have selected from it only those principles and ideas that can be put to practical use.

No longer can any person in business or the professions say: "Psychology is of no use to me. It cannot help me to earn more money or to develop my abilities."

I have prepared a list of 20 practical questions. To answer them, some knowledge of the New Psychology is needed:

1. How can I develop my abilities quickly?
2. How can the intelligence and usefulness of employees be enhanced?

3. How can I create the right conditions for thinking?

4. Are there any stimulants to boost one's mental capacity?

5. How can I avoid a mental breakdown?

6. Can I learn to make decisions more quickly and wisely?

7. How can I learn to make good judgments?

8. How can I acquire a better understanding of human nature?

9. What is the right attitude towards people who are abnormal?

10. How can I win favorable attention to myself and my business?

11. How can I keep up with changes in the world?

12. How can I distinguish between what is true and what is false?

13. What benefit can I derive from reading novels?

14. What benefit can I derive from travel?

15. How can I draw strength from the emotional influences of my life?

16. How can I overcome defects of temperament?

17. How far is it possible to avoid the habit of worrying?

18. How can I master fear?

19. How can my home-life assist me in achieving my goals?

20. How can I get more of the joys of life in the midst of my work?

In the following chapters you will find the answers to these questions. And the answers, taken as a whole, will, I hope, give you a fairly clear idea of what is meant by the New Psychology.

HERBERT N. CASSON

CHAPTER 1

The Main Thing is Self-Development

The New Psychology teaches us to know more about the ideas, motives and feelings of ourselves and others. It concentrates attention on the inner life - on the mental and emotional causes of action. And its most valuable service is this - that it helps people to develop their own mental powers and to control the feelings that weaken them.

"Know thyself" - that is a theme of the New Psychology. The moment young people get ambitious, they must begin to examine and develop all their latent power and talent to enable them to succeed. And when older people realize that they are not making any headway, they should immediately take stock of their strong and weak points and make a fresh start. Is it not true that many people in business are so concerned with making a success of their business that they have no time to think of themselves? They consider themselves as finished products - they have nothing more to learn about themselves. This is a disastrous mistake.

All through their business careers they may be held back by some lack of knowledge or some temperamental defect. They may be great believers in the improvement and up-dating of equipment, yet they may wholly neglect the improvement of their own mental and temperamental equipment, which is of more importance than all else. To those who find themselves caught in the whirl of a successful and growing business, I would say: "Now and then stop and give a thought to YOURSELF. What are YOU getting out of it? Are you, too, growing? Are you gaining in knowledge and happiness?"

An American poet once wrote these verses, which people would do well to ponder:

"We are all blind until we see
That in the human plan
Nothing is worth the making if
It does not make the man.

Why build these cities glorious
If man unbuilded goes?
In vain we build the work, unless
The builder also grows."

All people in business should watch out for this danger signal:

When the person at the head of a growing business does not himself grow, his business is in danger.

How often do we see a business shoot up like a rocket and come crashing down in little pieces! Why? Because the person at the top of the business was not big enough to handle it when it began to grow rapidly. The business flopped because the big boss did not know how to organize, how to plan and how to cope with expansion. He remained small while his business grew big.

A growing business can also fail because the person at the top has no self-control. Such a person is liable to throw caution to the wind and is soon deep in trouble.

Sudden success sometimes makes people money-mad. They become unprincipled and ruthless, and plunge headlong into a mad race to make more money with renewed ferocity. In such cases it would be much better for them, their families and their businesses if they take things in their stride. Their success and wealth can turn them into nasty people.

I have no doubt that the first duty of people in business is to develop themselves. Many people allow themselves to be mastered by their business and in the process may lose their health, good qualities and peace of mind. Their problems invariably become too complicated and difficult for them to solve.

When they reach the stage where they are no longer interested in their own development, there is no hope for them. They may make a good start and survive on a bit of luck, but they will never make any business grow big and stay big.

Big jobs require big people. At least, in the business world they do. Small people may remain in high positions in politics, but will never last long in business. It matters little whether or not you are making a lot of money, the most important thing in the world to you should be YOURSELF.

No one, not even the most egotistical person, would be brazen enough to say in public: "I am perfect." Yet, there are many who act as though they know everything there is to know. They stop learning and think that anyone who has the courage to disagree with them is a fool. They sometimes attribute to themselves the infallibility of a god. They never seem to know or care what idiots they make of themselves by this pose of omniscience except, perhaps, at the end of their days when they look back on their lives and realize the mistakes they made.

Everyone has defects. Some are inherited and some acquired. Even the wisest person does not know everything. Life is too short to learn all that there is to know. There are about 400,000 words in the English language, and not many of us know more than 20,000 or 30,000. All of us have some latent abilities that have never been developed. The average person, research has shown, uses less then a tenth of the potential output of his brain.

Let's assume a young person has inherited a 100-acre farm. He looks over the farm briefly and decides to use only ten acres around the farmhouse, leaving the other 90 acres to deteriorate. You would be right in thinking that young person a fool. Yet this is exactly what the average person does with his brain. I don't think I would be too far off the mark in saying that the majority of people have what can be called ten-per-cent brains. In other words, they use only one-tenth of their brains.

People must make the development of their brains a top priority in their lives. Latent abilities are worthless unless developed. And the only way to do this is first to develop the brain. The value or worth of people's brains lies in how well they make use of them.

They must first make a study of their aptitudes. Then find out what they can do best and most easily. They must come up with a purpose, then systematically gather knowledge, gain experience and develop every latent ability that will help them to achieve their purpose.

They must take control of themselves, stop being pushed about and drifting aimlessly. They may have to form new habits and reach out to a new set of more intelligent and helpful friends. They may have to cut loose from quite a few people and quite a few habits. Those who want to make the grade must expect to leave a good deal behind.

There must be a crisis of DECISION. Merely wishing, hoping and dreaming helps no one. There must come a time for some people when they value the future more than the present. As

4

soon as they do this, they will be willing to pay the price for their self-development. They will take themselves in hand and make whatever changes are necessary to their progress.

After the decision comes the QUEST - the quest for the knowledge and experience that is needed. In the case of wise, ambitious people, this quest never ends while life lasts. In the case of most people, however, it never begins. People cannot develop their abilities unless they are teachable, and they cannot go far unless they retain the curiosity of childhood to learn everything about the new things that come along.

People can gain a certain amount of knowledge - a small amount - from their friends and associates. But if what they know is no more than what their friends or associates know, then they will stand little chance for advancement. Their problem will then be: How to stand out among the crowd, how to become distinctive. To do so, they must make it a point to seek knowledge elsewhere.

The quickest way to do this is to cultivate the reading habit. No matter what a person's job or purpose is, he can learn much from books. It is no longer true that book-knowledge has no practical value. Today, books crammed with information and knowledge on any subject you can think of, are available to those who take the time and trouble to find them. And they are affordable, too. In fact, most of them can be found in libraries. Most large business corporations have well-stocked libraries of their own. There are a lot of self-made people around who owe their success to the fact that they loved, and still love, to read.

People can also improve themselves by attending adult education classes at night, taking correspondence courses or part-time polytechnic or university courses if they have the minimum educational requirements necessary.

After dealing with the quest, attention must be focused on a CAMPAIGN OF ACTION. People must be able to DO things as well as learn them. The best way to achieve this is to do something creative every day. The creative thing may be either an act or a thought. The brain must be conditioned to produce creative ideas. People must make themselves thinkers as well as readers. It would be pointless to merely absorb what has been read and repeat it in parrot fashion. People's brains must be more than organs to memorize things with. They must be workshops to challenge ideas and concepts, reject them if need be and come up with new ideas.

This is the most striking difference between the psychology of yesteryear and today - the old was static whereas the new is dynamic. According to the old point of view, there need not be any campaign of action. A hermit could retire to a secluded home, sit down with his books and proceed to make himself an authority on psychology.

The study of psychology today means developing a creative brain and observing the behavior of other people. First, we must get to know ourselves very well. Then we must find out how to influence the opinions of others. That is my definition of the New Psychology.

It is not a suitable subject of study for philosophers or hermits. The right way to learn how to swim is by going into the water, not by making motions with your hands on land. The way to learn how the brain works is to USE it, not to memorize theories. And the way to find out the real principles of psychology is to gather data on the ideas, feelings and actions of as many people as possible.

The New Psychology is a study that never ends - a study that is always offering some new and useful point of interest. As long as we live, we can learn from the study of how our own minds function, from books and from the behavior of others. It will lead us far afield, but we must never forget that when we set out to learn the New Psychology, we must begin with OURSELVES.

CHAPTER 2

Helping to Develop Your Employees

This chapter will answer the question: "How can I increase the intelligence, usefulness and loyalty of my employees?" This is a question that should constantly occupy the minds of all employers. Those who are not interested in it have no business employing anyone.

Employers must be far more than just bosses. They must be people-trainers if they want to build up organizations that will continue to function long after they are gone. To build up an organization merely on blind obedience to you alone as an employer is to build it on a foundation of sand. Businesses created by strong but unwise people, whose only aim appears to be to make themselves indispensable, will quickly fall to pieces when they die.

Wise employers are as keen to develop their employees as they are to develop themselves. Their problem is not to see how much of the work they can do themselves, but to see how much of it can be well done by their employees. Here we have the main reason for staff training.

When an employer uses psychology in dealing with his employees, he is forced to think of the human element. This leads him to eliminate any harsh or unfair features that may exist in his method of management.

A manufacturer who takes an interest in psychology does not think in terms of having at his disposal "2000 hands." Rather, he is inclined to say to himself: "I have 1000 brains working for me. All of them have various opinions and feelings. How can I make my people more contented and more useful?" He is acutely aware that what the people in his organization think and feel is a matter of vital importance.

A managing director does not and should not give direct orders to rank and file employees. But he must and should concern himself with what they do, what they know and under what conditions they work. Most of the routine work of any organization consists of small jobs done by small people. In even the smallest job there is a element of skill. Consequently, there must be a system to show employees how to do their jobs. They must not be left to learn from one another. And they must be taught to believe that their top bosses are sincerely interested in their welfare and happiness.

Ideas on efficient organization are changing. Long ago the emphasis was placed on system. But over the years, bosses have learned to rely more on initiative. It has been found that system is likely to develop into bureaucracy. It is apt to become mere routine, with no attention paid to the vital matter of net profit.

We have also found out the weak side of supervision. We have learned the futility of merely making rules to police a body of workers. We have found it far better to first give the workers complete instructions that will put them in the right frame of mind to work with loyalty and efficiency. With a few exceptions here and there, we have found that people can be trusted to a far greater extent than was thought possible by employers two generations ago.

The concept of "management-sharing" is being adopted more and more. Managements are now routinely asking even rank and file workers to send in suggestions relating to various aspects of their work and working conditions. In short, they are being asked to THINK. Competent top and middle management are now encouraging their subordinates to take on more responsibilities. Authority is much less monopolized than it used to be.

There is a strong tendency towards decentralization. We have found that centralization has many disadvantages. It makes a firm slower and more bureaucratic. It prevents routine from being flexible. We have found that it is possible to carry standardization too far. We are giving a larger measure of liberty and initiative to branch managers and so on.

When an employer sets out to train his staff, he should begin with a nucleus of his most highly paid people. Contrary to the general opinion, staff training should begin at the top. By means of weekly conferences and a series of lectures now and then, the people at the top of the business should be stimulated to continue their education and to co-operate more effectively with one another.

Then the task of training the rank and file should be turned over to the heads of departments. It is better, in my opinion, to decentralize the training. When heads of departments are bypassed, they are not likely to approve of the training or cooperate with the instructors.

There should, of course, be a system of promotion by merit, not by seniority. This stimulates hope and ambition. Companies should be loyal to their old employees, but they should not risk being slowed down by making age the main qualification or criteria for promotion. If they do, they will inevitably lose their most ambitious and competent young people.

A little thought should be given to the so-called "dead end" jobs. There are many such jobs and employers should consider their psychological effects because they can turn employees into robots. Employers should try not to tie down their workers to such jobs indefinitely.

One of the principles of efficiency is the giving of incentives. As far as possible, both executive and non-executive staff should be paid on results, as should managing directors, in my opinion.

Salesmen will do more if they are given commission as well as small salaries. Incentives can be given for outstanding work. If an employee makes an extra £100 over and above his sales quota for the company, he should certainly be entitled to £10 of it. The giving of incentives keeps employees alert and enthusiastic. It gives them a partner's interest in their company.

There should be company libraries stocked with not only books providing light reading, but books on business and the other professions as well. The primary purpose of a library is to educate and inform. Its secondary purpose is to entertain. Libraries also enable bosses to discover those employees who are keen on self-improvement and who are possible promotion prospects.

One method of developing the most competent young people in a company is to organize - to appoint - promising employees to a junior or minor board of directors to see how well they perform. This board could be a testing ground for future appointments to top posts in the organization.

I am going to turn to Japan for the best example of the value of a policy of staff training. The famous "House of Mitsui" adopted this policy about three centuries ago. As a result, it became one of the largest financial, industrial and commercial organizations in Japan.

It controls huge companies, and owned, as long ago as the 1930s, the largest store in the Far East. It produces steel, coal, rubber, chemicals, rayon, cotton cloth, etc. It builds houses. It has tea plantations. It owns steamships. More than any other group, it has influenced the industrial and commercial development of Japan.

The founder of the organization drew up a company code: Here are a few of its precepts:

The members of the "House of Mitsui" should deal with one another in close friendship and with kindness.

Practise thrift but avoid luxury, which ruins a man.

Employ men of great abilities and make full use of their special talents.

Replace the aged and decrepit with young men of promise.

Our house has its own enterprises; never touch an outside business.

Make your sons begin with the mean tasks of apprentices, and learn management in branch houses. He who does not know cannot lead.

The amazing success and stability of this Mitsui company compels us to notice the value of a code - the value of a body of instruction. Surely every other large company should also have its own system of education and character-building. It should make its success certain and permanent by developing all its employees - by constantly improving the human element as well as the equipment.

CHAPTER 3

Right Conditions for Thinking

This subject of right conditions for thinking is one that is almost ignored in most books on psychology, but it is certainly worth devoting a whole chapter to. In both mental and physical activity we must do our best to secure favorable conditions for them.

All ambitious people are interested in this question: "How can I create the right conditions to give my brain a chance to give of its best?" There are not many people, I suspect, who could truthfully say at the end of their lives: "I have made the best possible use of my mental powers."

It is not often that the average person relishes the thought of putting on, as we say, his "thinking cap". It is also not often that he even notices how he even dislikes to think. There are probably lots of people who can say to themselves at the end of a week: "I have had no mental net profit during the past week as I have not given a single hour to thinking."

In spite of the fact that the success of any business depends most of all on thinking, most of us do not spend one quarter as much time on thinking as we do on correspondence. We are likely to stamp "Urgent" on our non-thinking jobs and "Not Urgent" on our thinking jobs.

I would not be surprised if there are some people in business who are quite proud to say: "I have no time to think." To this the appropriate reply is: "What can be more important than thinking?" Many people allow themselves to be overwhelmed by details. They get caught up in endless routine. They are too busy with trifles. They get the false notion that it is a good thing to be occupied in that manner. Later in life they will probably wake up to the fact that it is not a wise policy to be too busy to think.

People must keep their eyes open while they are walking, otherwise they might hurt themselves by falling into a drain or being knocked down by a car crossing the street. They must also keep their brains active even in the midst of routine work, otherwise they might vegetate. If they neglect to do both, they could end up becoming robots. The tendency of all routine work is to dull and deaden the mind, resulting in the brain ceasing to observe what is going on around it. There must be a conscious effort to keep the brain active.

The job of a salesman, for instance, gives far better conditions for thinking than the job of a clerk. He or she is almost free from routine work. Sales people learn to develop thick skins and must carry on despite all the difficulties and all the rebuffs. They meet all sorts of people. In such a situation, they are compelled to think.

Bosses who sit in their offices for the better part of the day need to set aside a certain amount of time once or twice a week in a quiet place for creative thinking. There should not be any interruptions. Some chief executives take one or two top aides with them on these "thinking" sessions.

Some big organizations have special "think tanks" - chalets or bungalows - beside the sea or some mountain resort precisely for this purpose. When some big reorganization is planned or a takeover bid is on the cards, top executives spend a week or two at these "hideaways" planning strategies. Now and again, chief executive officers retire to these place simply to get an overview or "bird's-eye" view of their business and its problems from a distance - far from the hustle and bustle of routine work.

There are some people who can think clearly even in the midst of distractions. They have this remarkable ability to detach their minds from everything around them and concentrate on whatever it is they want to think about. There are, however, not many people who have this gift of being wholly indifferent to outside influences.

Everyone can develop the power to concentrate. They can learn to focus or direct their minds on to a certain line of thought without deviating from it. A mind that flits here and there will, of course, find it very difficult to think things through to their logical conclusion. The value of people's thinking depends to a large extent on their mood at the moment. We know that if people are in a happy mood, they are likely to buy things at inflated prices. But if they are in a pessimistic or sad mood, they are likely to sell things at very low prices. A mood creates a mental climate. It may make clear thinking easier or more difficult.

A very useful rule to remember is this - never make an important decision when in a fit of depression. Such a rule could save lots of people from making foolish and perhaps tragic decisions. Whenever people are depressed, the weaker part of their minds are in control. Circumstances arise that for a time overwhelm them.

At such a time they should say to themselves: "This mood will pass. I must endeavor to let the more positive elements in my brain take control. And I must not make any decision until I return to normal again."

The brain is often put temporarily out of order and becomes

fuzzy and disorientated when people are intoxicated. Too many alcoholic drinks arouses the latent animalism in people. For a time they cease to be rational human beings. They may become in turn jolly, sad, boisterous, quarrelsome or extremely violent. Some like to sing, cry or fall asleep.

This mental state happens too, when emotions like anger, jealously, fear or grief take temporary control of the mind. And each emotion is capable of triggering different reactions in different people. It is like a full-scale storm or tornado of irresistible feelings that sweep through the mind.

Will power is for a time over-powered. At such times there can be no clear thinking. And no decisions should be made until the will power regains control.

It goes without saying that we should do everything we can to avoid unnecessary worry, because it creates a mental block, shackles the mind and prevents clear thinking.

Emotionally-speaking, there are three categories of people: the happy-go-lucky few who never seem to worry at all; those who worry only when they NEED to; and those who worry over everything - the ones whose lives are one big worry. It is the last category that should be warned about worrying unnecessarily. Some of them foolishly believe that worrying is a form of thinking. To think is to be positive, to be creative, while worry brings about just the opposite effect. No one is silly enough to throw sand under the bonnet of his car, but there are many who acquire the habit of clogging up their minds with worry. Result in both cases - total breakdown.

The process of thinking is also disturbed by ill health. Scientists are finding out more and more about the marvellous relationship between brain and body. A thought can cause illness. It can also help to bring about a cure. Creative thinking is hampered by pain and often by bodily ailments. To obtain the best conditions for thinking, the body must be in good working order. It's possible for people to have healthy and well-developed bodies and yet to not be able to think. They may have foundations and no superstructures; but they are not likely to have safe superstructures without the foundations.

It is an odd fact that many people think best only at certain times of the day. Some people produce their best work only in the morning before noon. If they are authors or composers that's the time of the day they feel they are the most productive. Others find they cannot be creative until the sun goes down. People who are creative must discover for themselves when they can do their best thinking. This is indeed food for thought.

We know that a gardener has to create the right conditions in a garden before he can get the best results out of it. He must make sure that the soil is good - there must be enough nutrients for the plants to grow well. Stones and weeds must be removed and there must be enough rain and sunshine. Finally, the best quality and type of seeds must be purchased if the garden is to look beautiful.

We also know that the right conditions are necessary for workers in an office or factory if they are to give of their best. There must be plenty of light where needed, the right temperature, rest-room, cafeteria and toilet facilities etc. These are some of the basic working conditions required, not to mention annual leave, free medical attention and hospitalization, insurance coverage for certain jobs, maternity and compassionate leave, gratuity, pension, car and housing loans.

It is equally true that right conditions are necessary for the brain just as they are for a garden, office or factory. The duty of everyone is to give his or her brain a fair chance to do its best.

CHAPTER 4

The Stimulation of the Brain

This chapter answers an important question: "Are there any stimulants to boost one's mental capacity?"

The word "stimulant" is often misused by being applied only to alcoholic drinks, which do stimulate or create geniality and an artificial sense of well-being. But no one has yet proved or, I believe, even tried to prove, that they stimulate or help in the process of thinking.

The use of opium, hashish, morphine, cocaine and other such drugs does have a strong effect on the brain, but not at all a beneficial one. They do create an exaggerated feeling of well-being in the beginning, but do absolutely nothing to stimulate thought. Rather, they slowly and systematically destroy it. They induce hallucinations in seasoned drug addicts and the after-effects worsen with each succeeding dose. These so-called "stimulants" bring nothing but misery and wretchedness.

Smoking does tend to slow down the brain, but it has a soothing effect and gives a perceptible sense of well-being. It appears to decrease worry and irritability for the addict. Some may argue that smoking has a beneficial effect on the brain and may increase a person's output. But the health hazards of the smoking habit outweigh any "benefits" it bestows on the smoker.

We know that drinking tea or coffee does stimulate the brain with no bad after-effects. People who drink a strong cup of tea or coffee just before making a speech will find that their brains become keener and more active. A heavy meal has the opposite effect - it makes the brain sluggish.

The best of all brain stimulants is to have a worthwhile purpose. When people's lives are aimless, they begin to deteriorate. Their eyes become dull, they do their work mechanically and most of their attention is concentrated on pleasures. People with idle minds constantly require to be entertained and, like children, they are constantly seeking amusement.

Many people, mainly rich and young, are bored stiff with life. Uppermost in their minds is this question: "Where can we go next to have some fun?"

They are not happy unless they are going to a movie, a party, a discotheque or up to some mischief like taking drugs. They seldom derive any happiness or satisfaction from simple pleasures. The moment the fun is over, they relapse into boredom.

Their never-ending wish is : "If only I had more money." Even if they get their wish, it is not likely to help them much because they get only a fleeting pleasure from what they buy. You may have noticed that when rich people buy three or four luxurious mansions, they usually wind up living in a hotel or on a yacht.

From the point of view of efficiency, being "fed up" with life is a serious matter. To be efficient, one must first be interested in one's work and self-development. The secret of success and happiness is to be entertained and satisfied by whatever we are doing, and not merely by shows, cruises, movies, wild parties, etc.

No one can derive solid satisfaction, on which happiness is based, unless he is interested in his work, enjoys his home life and strives to fulfill some worthwhile purpose. Anyone who can do this will never be bored with life. And anyone who thinks of others as well as himself, will always find life interesting.

The state of mind that should be avoided at all cost is that of APATHY. When people arrive at the stage when they say: "What's the use? I don't care," there is little hope for them. They become one of the unburied dead.

A wise old author once wrote: "If there is a pitiable object in the whole universe, it is a misplaced person who has lost his ambition, who has ceased to care whether he goes up or down, who is indifferent to his future. A watch is of no use without a mainspring. All the other wheels and hands and mechanism are useless without that which will move them. When ambition is dead there is no hope for the person unless ambition can be revived; and it is very difficult to arouse a dead ambition."

Even people who have sunk to the depths of apathy can sometimes be aroused - resurrected - and brought back to the land of the living. When they are discouraged, they must be quick to shake off their discouragement, before it leads to apathy. They must take action and begin to find a purpose in life to fulfill.

Generally, people begin to slow down between the ages of 55 and 65. They must, of course, slow down physically between those ages, but there is no good reason why they should slow down mentally as well.

The fact is that the brain, if it is properly stimulated, can be at its best after 55. Many people discover, much to their surprise, that brains are twice as active at 60 as they were at 30.

One of the best ways to keep the brain active is to develop the power of observation. If the eyes are sharp and observant, they will keep the brain busy. Anyone who has lived in the same house and worked at the same job for some years is inclined to let himself get into a rut. His powers of observation will decrease considerably. He arrives at a point where he sees only what is sensational or unusual. This is what happens when no special effort is made to constantly sharpen one's powers of observation.

Anyone from 15 to 90 who can retain a little of the natural curiosity of children - that desire to observe and question everything - will never lose the ability to think clearly.

Hope and ambition, too, stimulate the brain. That is why young people should be encouraged and not repressed when they wish to express themselves. The self-confidence of the young is like a tender plant. It can easily be uprooted. Ever since the human race inhabited the earth, the elderly have been telling the young what they can or cannot say. No doubt they will go on doing so till the end of time.

A lot of older people forget that children and youngsters need to be encouraged and praised - to feel wanted. People of mature age usually know what they want. They are not easily influenced by what other people say or do. But children or youngsters have not as yet developed such self-confidence. A thoughtless word here or there can scar them for life. As a rule, children or young people will go that extra mile only if they are treated with kindness and encouraged to do so.

The mind is also stimulated by intelligent conversation. Young people can seldom talk freely with people twice their age. Consequently, they find it more convenient and wiser to move around with people in their age group, preferably with similar interests and backgrounds. Idle conversation, which requires little or no thinking, does nothing to stimulate the mind.

Perhaps the most useful of all brain-stimulants is READING. There is a lot of trash on book-shelves and news stands today, but it is also true that never before has there been so many useful and instructive books and magazines. With all that material available at libraries and a good book being within the reach of everyone's pocket, it has become possible for anyone desiring to do so to acquire a fairly comprehensive knowledge on any subject, if the habit of reading is cultivated.

Carrying out experiments is one of the best ways to stimulate the brain into action. It compels the brain to be creative. To begin the process, people should always "suppose" something. They should say to themselves: "Suppose I do this or that, what will happen? Will I improve things or make them worse? This desire to try to improve things is one of the most valuable habits to cultivate.

So this business of keeping the brain busy requires some extra special attention. The status of a nation is decided by the quality and quantity of its top thinkers. And no loss is more devastating to a nation, especially one with little or no natural resources, than a brain-drain of its able thinkers.

CHAPTER 5

How to Prevent Brain-Fag

I can assure you that it is not a pleasant experience to see a healthy person become the victim of a mental breakdown. Sometimes the breakdown is only temporary, in which case a victim can recover sufficiently to become his or her normal self. But sometimes, the condition becomes irreversible and leads to permanent loss of sanity.

Business people who fall victim to this terrible malady can be found in spas, nursing homes and in hospitals for the mentally ill everywhere you go. I think it is an accepted fact that, given the highly stressful lives that people lead today, not nearly enough is being done to alleviate or remedy the situation.

We often give the most careful attention and consideration to the preservation of our material and financial assets, and yet act like fools when it comes to keeping our mental assets in tip-top condition. This is a very common phenomenon in business life. Those who regard themselves as hard-headed and efficient in business affairs will scoff at the idea of turning to psychology to help them cope with the stress, strain and worry in their work. Instead, they permit themselves to plunge headlong towards a mental breakdown.

People in business generally don't look after themselves well. They drive themselves too hard and they take better care of their machines than of themselves. They over-estimate their mental capacity for punishment. Most of them are far too tense. They probably go to sleep with their teeth and fists clenched. Work to them is a matter of life and death.

When people set out to build a business, they must certainly work hard, but they need not mix their blood with the mortar. They must remember that the brain is a delicate and complex organ. They must obey certain rules. They will lose nothing by working wisely, pacing themselves to suit their mental capacities. If they obey the rules that relate to the well-being of their minds, they will accomplish far more and save themselves the misery of a breakdown.

People should work no more than eight or nine hours a day and not 12 to 14. They should not fall into the habit of taking work home at night. They need the evenings for rest, for home life and recreation. If they work until bedtime, they will not be at their best the next morning, because they will hardly get any sleep, and sound sleep is the best medicine for an over-worked brain.

It is not so much the extra work that hurts them as the mood of worry and near desperation in which it is done. They go home with grim faces, carrying briefcases filled with business papers, and the first words their families hear are: "This work MUST be finished by tonight." Then they shut themselves in a room for two or three hours, issue orders that the children must be quiet and proceed to slog.

Their extra work would not tire them much if they came home in a cheerful frame of mind and said: "We were very busy today," played with their children after supper, worked for an hour, relaxed with their wives for a while and then worked for a second hour.

Of course, the effect on their minds would be much more disastrous if they spent their evenings in dissipation. They would then be "burning the candle at both ends". To work hard all day and then to spend half the night dancing, drinking or gambling is the surest way to a mental breakdown.

Then there are people who almost literally attack their work. The same spirit is carried over into their play and amusements. They are people of exceptional energy. They awake in the morning with a bound and dress as though the house was on fire.

Such people often accomplish a great deal, but sooner or later they could end up in a "double-barrelled" breakdown - of the body as well as the mind. They forget that the body is like a tank that stores energy and it must be replenished with more energy before it is used again, otherwise the whole system breaks down.

The mind and body require relaxation. It has been found that the output or productivity of a factory can be increased by giving the workers a short rest period in the middle of the morning and in the middle of the afternoon. Work is inclined to slow down just before the mid-day break, pick up again after it and slow down again just before work ends for the day.

From experience and observation, I believe that people who do mental work should work in two-hour periods. A person's brain will work at high speed for two hours. Then it begins to slow down because it needs at least a half-hour of relaxation. Any mental work done when the brain is fatigued is not likely to be well done.

People who do a lot of thinking should take up hobbies that help their minds to relax. Many such people keep themselves mentally fit by doing a lot of gardening or some other activity that involves little or no thinking at all.

It is dangerous to be in debt to nature. We must pay our dues for what she provides - not in 30 or 60 days, but every day. At the end of every night's sleep we must have had enough rest and enough energy to prepare us to face the problems of a new day. If a person uses up 100 units of energy a day and takes in only 80 to tackle the next day, that means a debt of 20 units is owed to Mother Nature. If this goes on indefinitely, there will soon be a big overdraft that the person will find very difficult, if not impossible, to settle. In business, too large an overdraft could mean bankruptcy. When it comes to health, however, it could mean death.

Make a single day the unit of measurement for whatever you do. If this rule is strictly obeyed, it would, in my opinion, prevent brain-fag. Whenever a day's work has been especially tiring, spend a bit more time in recreation or sleep. Make every day pay for itself. Put back as much energy as has been expended - more if you can but never less.

To everyone who has heavy responsibilities, I would say: "Delegate some of your lesser responsibilities to your subordinates. There is a limit to what one person can do. The larger a business is, the less routine work should be done by the person at the top. Cut free as far as possible from the daily routine and devote your energy to planning for the future."

People should not take on new duties until they have set aside enough time to attend to them without extending themselves unnecessarily. If they try to cram 15 hours' work into ten hours, the work will suffer and so will they. Anyone can safely overwork himself for a brief period, but if he makes it a habit, he will soon be brought to a standstill. There is a limit to what the mind can take. This limit must never be exceeded. A proper balance in lifestyle must be maintained to allow the mind to work energetically, and to make the decisions required.

CHAPTER 6

How to Make Probably Correct Decisions

There is no known method of always making the correct decisions. The mind is not at all like a laboratory. It does not deal with things that are definitely known. It is fed with a jumble of facts, traditions, opinions and all sorts of other information, then puts on its thinking cap, sifts through them and arrives at a decision.

Therefore, the most that people can expect when they make decisions is to accept the fact that they will PROBABLY, not DEFINITELY, be correct. It is important to remember this because a lot of people waste so much precious time unable to make up their minds on anything because they are afraid they will make the WRONG decision.

In order to make a quick decision, one must first develop the will and desire to do so. Unless a person is prepared to take the responsibility for his actions AND his decisions, he will never pluck up enough courage to say "yes" or "no" decisively when he is asked to make up his mind. He will, at best, play second fiddle to the leader of the orchestra.

A good many people are content to just drift along, relying on others to make decisions for them. This sort of person is referred to as "one of the crowd". People who have a goal in life and do something to achieve it are few and far between.

There are some, especially the young ones, who are always wishing they could have this or that, or do this or that. They envy others their positions, wealth and pleasures. They ask themselves: "Why can't I have the good things in life others have? Why do some people have all the luck?" Unfortunately, these people do nothing to make their dreams come true. And the simple reason is because they lack the determination and the will to do it. It is a good thing for young people to wish for better things. Wishes are like seeds. Every successful career probably started with a wish. No one however, has succeeded in getting wishes cashed at a bank. Seeds are of no value until planted, so wishes are also of no value until the wisher has the will and the purpose to get what he or she wants.

So the ability to assert one's will and make up one's mind swiftly is indispensable when it comes to making quick decisions. Practice makes perfect, they say. So the best way is to set out to learn something, do something or improve something in whatever way you want to and in the time you set yourself to do it.

Asserting one's will is a creative function. You use the power of your will to make the decision to do something. With practice comes self-confidence which, in turn, will help to erase any doubts or feelings of inferiority. Soon the ability to make quick decisions will no longer be difficult.

The thing to remember, however, is that asserting one's will in order to make quick decisions is one thing, but making sure that the decisions are not only practical but wise is another thing. This is where will-power - the ability to control one's actions, emotions and impulses - comes into play. The development of will-power helps considerably in keeping a check on the arbitrary assertiveness of one's will in making unwise decisions.

It is will-power, plus perseverance, that makes dreams of success come true, not always, but often enough. Few people accomplish everything they set out to do, but more of us can achieve some of the things we set our hearts on, if we have the courage and determination to pay the price for them.

Quite a few business people have great difficulty making decisions. There is always a debate going on in their minds between the "pros" and "cons" of everything they are asked to decide on. There is nothing really wrong with wanting to look at problems from every angle. But these people clutter up their minds with "pros and cons" that have no bearing whatsoever, on the matter at hand. In short, they can't see the wood for the trees.

Take a look at the desks of some executives and you will probably find them littered with deferred matters. Their businesses suffer because they cannot make decisions quickly. It may be better and, perhaps, more profitable for such people to make decisions on the flip of a coin. They are like drivers who stop their cars instantly at traffic inter-sections even before the amber lights come on. They freeze up and begin to panic for no reason at all.

Problems are bound to crop up during and after the planning of anything. Perhaps the problems will turn out to be so insurmountable that it would not be worthwhile proceeding with the project. Or they may be relatively minor, in which case, the go-ahead to proceed with the work can be given. In any case, the decision either way cannot be made until all the relevant factors have been taken into account and all the risks and advantages have been fully considered.

Of course, no one can be 100 per cent correct all the time. This does not mean, however, that everyone should be afraid to make decisions because they might make mistakes. A business must go on and the people in charge of it must be able to make many decisions each day. And often, they don't have the time in which to do so.

Important decisions, however, should not be made over-hastily. One effective rule that helps to prevent the making of unwise decisions is never to say "yes" or "no" on any important matter without first making sure you agree with the CAUSE or MOTIVE that prompts the decision. Even in the business world, far too many people make decisions or take action based on misinformation, gossip, prejudices and so on. And when a person's decisions are influenced merely by such causes or motives, most of them will turn out to be unwise decisions.

Wise people look carefully into the reasons for their actions. They weigh the "pros" and "cons" assiduously, and they don't come to hasty conclusions based purely on hearsay. They don't sell their shares in Blank Ltd, simply because someone on the train said to them: "I think Blank Ltd is in for a hard time."

Neither do they decide not to buy computers for the office because their office managers think it would be wiser to buy adding machines first. Perhaps their office managers may have a personal dislike for computers. They will not sack someone because his superior has said something bad about him or her. That poor employee may be the victim of a grudge.

They do not reject a particular system outright merely because it is expensive or does not fit in with the life-styles of some executives. Big losses and a lot of ill-feeling can be avoided in business if people make it a point to ask themselves this question before saying "yes" or "no": "Are my reasons for making that decision good and fair enough?"

A thoughtful writer has come up with a method for making probably correct decisions in four steps as follows:

PROBABLY CORRECT DECISIONS

Observation and Fact-finding.
Defining the problem.
Study of possible solutions.
Decision.

CHAPTER 7

Judge by Facts and Results

"How can I make good judgments?" is a very interesting question which the New Psychology will endeavour to answer. There are five interrelated "musts" that go into the making of good judgments. First, people must try their best to develop judicial minds. Secondly, they must not make any decision detrimental to their own interests. Thirdly, they must not be swept off their feet by propaganda. Fourthly, they must be level-headed. And finally, they must remember to use their minds to weed out what is wise from what is foolish - what is true from what is false.

People should certainly be open to new methods and ideas. Those whose minds are not receptive to such ideas will not and cannot make good judgments. But what they must not do is believe, at face value, all that they read or all that they are told. They must be highly selective in digging up the facts and the truth. They must never permit rumour or gossip to influence them in any way. They must not let anyone make up their minds for them or allow their minds to become mere dumping grounds for others to exploit. And they must assert their independence to pass their own judgment on whatever they read or hear.

If people want to acquire the art of making good judgments, they must train themselves to distinguish facts from falsehoods. They must be able to see through the cunning schemes and deals offered by smooth-talking swindlers to unsuspecting dupes. Some of these swindlers are so adept at fooling people that it is very difficult to say "no" after their glib tongues have turned you into an ardent believer.

People should also be critical of both new and old ideas. An idea may be a thousand years old but it may not necessarily be a good one. By the same token, a new idea may appear to be most alluring and plausible but may turn out to be worthless or impracticable, perhaps even disastrous when it is tested.

A good rule is to judge everything by results. Whatever works well should be left alone. Whatever works badly should not be defended by opinions, feelings or prejudices. If a company makes no profits, its policy or management or both should be changed.

There is a big difference between faith and credulity. Faith means holding fast to the eternal principles of justice, integrity, goodness and truth. But credulity means that we are prepared to believe anything based on little or no evidence. It makes us the easy prey of demagogues, swindlers and charlatans.

Most people, at one time or another, have been guilty of being credulous. Credulity has obstructed the progress of science and civilization far more than most of us realize. It is credulity that fuels and strengthens superstition. Looking back on the history of the human race, there is nothing too absurd, harmful or brutal to be believed. Few people really check and test ideas before they accept them. Most of them are prepared to take at face value the most ridiculous things they are told.

One area where credulity is stretched to absurd lengths is in the business world. Confidence people continue to play the same old tricks with remarkable success. Very often there are reports in the newspapers of gullible people being swindled of small or large sums of money by such confidence tricksters. How many more cases go unreported will probably be never known.

A scam could work like this: A retiree meets a stranger at a party, who describes himself as a businessman in the import-export business. The stranger, who looks a decent sort, casually talks about the attractive investment opportunities in his line of business, and mentions, in passing, how much money others have made on their investments. The retiree rises to the bait and wants to know more about the scheme. So they agree to meet again a couple of days later when the stranger gets a firmer grip on his victim by making his investment schemes look even more attractive. Agreement is reached, so-called "papers" are drawn up and the victim soon sees his "gold mine" paying off regularly in high interest rates he cannot get elsewhere.

Soon, the retiree is itching to put more money into another "safe", attractive scheme. Of course, his "benefactor" is more than willing to accommodate him, and investment portfolio No.2 is finalized. Then a third and, perhaps, a fourth scheme is launched. By now, the victim is congratulating himself on being smart.

Some months later, the victim is offered the final "carrot" - a scheme requiring a large minimum investment over a four-month period offering even a higher interest rate. The retiree is given only a week to accept it. Naturally, he scrapes up all the loose change he has and dumps it in the scheme. And that is the last time he sees the swindler or a single penny of all the money he invested.

Countless people are taken in by various other con games, invariably using slightly different tactics. Incredible as it may seem, some of these people burn their fingers more than once. Obviously, they pay dearly to learn their lesson.

Perhaps the first great thinker who attacked credulity was seventeenth century French philosopher and mathematician Rena Descartes. It was he who pointed out the value of DOUBT. Briefly what he said is this - overhaul your beliefs and hold fast only to those that can be proved. Descartes was one of the earliest and most influential pioneers of rationalism, and his suggestions still have much practical value.

People who have money or property must be twice as good at doubting. Why? Because the world is full of predatory and parasitical people. It is not too difficult to make money these days, but it is beginning to become twice as easy to lose it with so many swindlers around.

In order not to lose the money you make these days, you need to develop a new set of qualities. Apart from caution and alertness, you need to remember that while a new scheme or project offers the chance to make some money, and easy money at that, it could easily turn out to be a scam to relieve you of it.

People should remember Descartes when they examine a company prospectus. They must read it carefully, and if they don't find the answers to any questions about the company in it, they should check elsewhere for them. And if there is any information about the company that does not add up, they should make it their business to know about it BEFORE and not AFTER they invest money in it.

Often there are advertisements in newspapers that read: "WANTED - a partner with £10,000. Those interested please contact so-and-so." Some advertisements do offer some worthwhile business opportunities to people with the capital to invest in them, but I would advise them to be extra careful about such offers. Even after sizing them up, it isn't wise to rush in where even seasoned business people "fear to tread", simply because they may be potential scams waiting for gullible victims to come along. Confidence tricksters will do anything to entice their victims.

Many people are very careless about investing money, and lose their first savings to swindlers. They buy or invest in things they know nothing about. The best rule for investors is this - stick to what you know well. Don't try to play another person's game. Vast amounts of money are lost by those who ignore this rule.

People should not fool themselves nor allow others to fool them. The best way to do that is to develop a judicious and analytical mind that will help you to make good, sound judgments.

CHAPTER 8

Constantly Study Human Nature

Psychology, more than anything else, helps one to find the answer to this question: "How can I have a better understanding of human nature?" After all, psychology is, according to the dictionary, the study of the human mind and human behaviour. There is little difference between the two except, perhaps, that psychology is generally used to refer to the mental and behavioural side of the human mind, and human nature is generally used to refer to the emotional side.

The New Psychology is not based on old metaphysical theories and classifications. It is based on the study of human nature, mental and emotional, in action. To get data, a keen interest must be taken in human behaviour, in how the mind operates and in the influence of the feelings upon action and belief.

As there is no way we can touch or see thoughts, feelings and character, we are compelled to notice the outward signs that will give us some information. Life is like a ball where everyone is in disguise. The disguises are never taken off. It is this unique fact that makes the study of human behaviour difficult.

An English poet once said: "The proper study of mankind is Man." Certainly there is no more useful study. It benefits shopkeepers and statesmen alike. Books provide knowledge to a certain degree. The rest has to be acquired through experience, by observation and by coming into contact with as many people as possible.

The study of human nature is a constant source of entertainment and instruction. It teaches us tolerance and respect for the views of others. It tends to influence others in a positive or negative way.

People who are sincerely interested in other people for what they are and not for what they can get out of them will eventually set out to serve them. They will have the right conception of their business, profession or any other activity.

There will always be some kind of human element present in problems business people encounter, either directly or indirectly. In spite of all the technological advances made, one indisputable fact stands out - success in any field of endeavour ultimately depends on people.

How a company performs depends on the people in it as well as those outside it who are persuaded to buy its goods and services. Governments, too, are composed of people, and no government can be any wiser than the people who run it.

Given the right leadership, a company grows and prospers. Given weak leadership, it will invariably sink lower and lower towards insolvency no matter how large its assets are. Behind every plan, idea, project, balance sheet or anything else in business you will find a person or a group of people. In short, business is people.

Business is mainly a matter of contacts - contacts with human nature. A person who has no self-control and only a limited knowledge of the art of dealing with people pleasantly is really not qualified to be in business in the first place. By sheer energy and ruthlessness, he may attain some measure of success, but not for long.

Internal friction has brought more than a few companies to a standstill. If the people in a company do not study and consider one another, the business is sure to suffer. When people in a company quarrel with one another, they are likely to quarrel with customers, too. The creation of goodwill begins INSIDE a company. That is a fact that many would-be business-builders forget.

A successful English manufacturer once said: "One of the main things in a business is atmosphere." He meant, of course, the mental conditions in a business. He meant opinions, manners, feelings, temperament and so on. There is such a thing as Weather in a business organization. There can be cloudy weather or bright sunshine or storms and thunder and lightning. Some businesses run pleasantly, while there is unpleasantness all day long, in others.

We place a great deal of emphasis upon being courteous to customers, but we do not pay half enough attention to being courteous to our business associates - to those who are working with us in the same company. When there is a genial, friendly atmosphere in a business organization, it makes a world of difference.

When people like their jobs and look forward to a working day, the effect on a company's profits can be electric. Yes, atmosphere at your place of work is a very important factor when it comes to gauging productivity. And everyone in a business organization, from the high and mighty to the humblest, helps to make the atmosphere what it is.

Some knowledge of human nature can be gained from books on character analysis and phrenology, but the main purpose served by books on these subjects is this - they teach us to be observant. We still do not know enough about human nature to really classify people and put them on shelves. Every rule that has been laid down has many exceptions.

The most practical and helpful study of human nature is the study of successful people. The principles of efficiency have been developed by studying the methods of the ablest business-builders. We tend to judge all methods by results. A method that has increased profits in one company is likely to be effective in other companies. In business as in sport, it is a wise policy to study the winners. Well-written biographies are a good source of information on behaviour.

Market research is an excellent way to find out the likes and dislikes of people and is an indispensable tool for business people in planning the types, quality and quantity of their products. This eliminates guess work and possible losses in producing goods that cannot be sold. Companies today spend a great deal of money on market research and use some elaborate systems to come up with statistics to guide them in their production strategies.

CHAPTER 9

Abnormal People

What can a boss do about employees who behave in an abnormal way? This is a question which I feel deserves a little chapter of its own. For instance, there are employees who are very capable but have one major fault. They cannot get along harmoniously with their associates in or outside the office. Apparently this is quite a common situation. And each case will invariably have its own peculiarities. But the basic reason for their behaviour can probably be attributed to one factor - a contempt for those not as smart as they are.

Such people are never satisfied unless they are criticizing or needling others - telling them how they should do their work. They are inconsiderate and can never bring themselves to work as a team. We often hear others say of such people: "They are extremely difficult to get on with." This is not because they are special or original in any way but because they are invariably trying desperately to hide something - possibly something about themselves they dislike so intensely that they consciously or unconsciously focus that dislike on others in the childish hope that it will go away. They probably believe that in making other people feel inferior they are somehow making up for whatever inadequacy it is that haunts them. Such people are inclined to be loners, and are difficult to get to know well or to talk with freely.

It may sometimes be due to a quirk in their temperament - a streak of contrariness or secretiveness. It's not what they say that makes others feel that way. It's simply their behaviour, their mannerisms. They lack the ability to make friends. Such people seldom succeed in their chosen work or profession.

People with outstanding abilities should certainly develop them to the fullest. Such abilities add considerably to their value - make them distinctive, even more so when they use them for the service of others.

There are centrifugal qualities in the brains of gifted people which could lead them to isolate themselves from others - to be self-centered and independent. Also there are other centripetal qualities which help people to be in touch with their contemporaries. It seems to me to be a wise and obvious policy for people to do their utmost to develop both qualities. They should cultivate the habit of thinking of others as well as themselves.

Employers who come across capable employees who cannot get along with their colleagues should try their best to get close to them. After all, such employees would be ideal if they could be persuaded to change their ways - their approach and attitude to other people. Employers should do everything in their power to draw them out and find out exactly what makes them behave that way. Only when they have exhausted all avenues to get to the root of the problem should they con-sider dispensing with their services. No one, no matter how brilliant, should be allowed to disrupt the team effort of a company or any other organization.

Elderly people, especially those who have had useful creative lives, can also become "difficult and peculiar". They may have a certain right to be described as "eccentric" because of their age and may be forgiven for not being able to "suffer fools gladly". They may have some unique characteristics and may well have earned the right in the twilight of their working years to be "difficult and peculiar". But people starting out or in the middle of their careers cannot offer this excuse for their peculiar behaviour.

In business life, we are compelled to deal with quite a few peculiar people, as employees or customers. Each one must be dealt with according to their peculiarities, but we must not allow them to disrupt things or shape our policies.

Let's take an example. An elderly woman walks into a shop. A sales girl greets her with a smile and says: "Good morning, madam." The woman replies frigidly: "I did not come into this shop to discuss the weather." It would clearly be a mistake if the owner of the shop decided to make a rule banning his sales people from smiling and saying: "Good morning".

Business rules are not like the formulae in a laboratory, because people are not like chemicals. In the making of these rules, the right policy is to cater to the normal - to trust to the law of averages. We should not disregard a rule merely because it is every now and then smashed by an exception.

Let's take the general rule: "The customer is always right." We know that there are quite a few exceptions to this rule. If a scientific study were made of customers' complaints, we might find that 30 per cent of them were not worth making all that fuss about. Even then, this rule would remain a wise one to follow because it insists upon retaining the goodwill of the customers.

CHAPTER 10

How to Win Favourable Attention

Many old-fashioned business people say: "Of what value is this New Psychology? How can it possibly be of any real use to us in our business?"

The best and quickest way to answer them is to say that it attracts favourable attention. I don't think they will deny that that is what they want above all else. And as soon as they begin to learn how to attract favourable public attention, they will have taken a plunge into psychology.

The selling of goods or services is a psychological problem. It is a matter of knowing how to make people notice us and think well of us. Every idea and method in use must be tested by the question: "What will be the psychological effect of it?" If it does not attract favourable attention, it may be considered a failure.

Now that we have entered the age of consumerism in a big way, the vital question that every company, factory, supermarket, department store and shop must try to answer is: "How can we make our business even more interesting?"

The answer to this question can be seen in the ever increasing advertising campaigns in newspapers, magazines and booklets, on television and billboards, at exhibitions and presentations and up in neon lights. Not to mention window display, which has been carried to new heights.

We have adopted methods of showmanship never dreamed of by our forefathers. Our department stores have become places of entertainment. Even conservative and old-established firms are making use of all sorts of sales gimmicks. Manufacturers vie with each other to come up with more attractive packaging. Industrial design is a business in itself. Why all this feverish activity? Simply to win the favourable attention of the public.

Many of the gimmicks and shows have no direct connection with the sale of goods. Their sole purpose is to attract attention. This reminds me of a contemporary of mine. On a very hot day, he placed a large block of ice in the foyer of his theatre. A friend said to him: "What is the use of that? It cannot cool the theatre." To which my friend replied: "I know that. But it looks so damned thoughtful."

The ever increasing advertising budget is due to several factors, not the least being vastly improved methods of production, increase in purchasing power and a wider variety and quantity of products flooding the market. Advertising is costly, but it costs less than guess-work or doing nothing but keeping your fingers crossed in the hope that your products will sell. Advertising agencies around the world have now become bigger and bigger and all their energies are directed towards one purpose - attracting the favourable attention of the public.

Lots of people have more needs and wants than the money with which to buy them. Consequently, in homes and smaller firms, there is much discussion on what to buy and not how much to buy. Large, prosperous companies simply buy what they want. So do wealthy people, but the less fortunate have to decide what they want MOST. For them it is a question of priority.

When poor families save a little money, they can think of 100 ways to spend it because there are so many things they need. But they can't afford to buy everything. They have to be selective. So they look up their priority list and buy what they need most badly. Their purchasing power is limited to basic necessities only, with little or nothing left over for luxury items.

So, here is where advertising, salesmanship and window display come in. They influence people who are making up their minds what to buy. In all our shops and department stores one article is competing with another for the favour of possible buyers. A striking window display may enable a woman to make up her mind. So may a skilled sales person. That is what salesmanship means - helping people to decide what to buy.

In retail selling, an elaborate structure of service has been built around the actual selling of the goods. The formula now is - every customer must be treated as a guest.

The first of several steps in making a sale is reception - the welcome of a customer. The last step is commendation - a word or two of thanks or approval after the sale has been completed. Neither of these has to do with the actual selling of the goods. They are designed to win the customer's favourable attention.

Salesmanship has been reconstructed from the point of view of what the customer thinks and feels. In short, it has been reconstructed with the aid of psychology. We are thinking now, not only of goods and prices, but of how to influence the mind of a possible customer and of the mental after-effect of a sale.

More stress is now laid on the personality of sales people, because they are usually the deciding factor in making sales. No matter how experienced they are in their sales pitch, their success or failure will ultimately depend on their personalities. We have found that above everything, people who sell things must be likable. They must be able to project a favourable image of themselves and must be congenial before they begin to sing the praises of the products they are selling.

At a hotel one evening, I spent some time before dinner watching people come in. I never did this before but it was worthwhile. Several people walked in, some of whom appeared to be salesmen. They spoke to no one. They were serious, tight-lipped men. Then a middle-aged man trooped in. He looked affable and friendly. With a broad grin he said to the head porter: "Good evening. Plenty of business, I see." He chatted and joked with the reception clerk. He spoke to the lift man, too. At dinner he struck up a conversation with the waitress and later spoke to a group of people for half an hour before disappearing into the writing room.

Later, I chatted with him and found him easy to talk to. He seemed to like people. He was a salesman - a successful one apparently, so the head porter told me the next morning. The point I want to make is this - he was exactly what every salesman ought to be. He made friends easily and had little difficulty drawing favourable attention to himself.

This tenth tip is equally important in management. Those in authority over others must ask themselves: "What is the attitude of people towards me? Do they speak about me in their homes? What do they say? Do they wish to please me? Have I succeeded in winning their favourable attention?"

Those who are familiar with the principles of efficiency know that the first thing a newly-promoted head of a company or department usually does is to secure the goodwill and cooperation of all the people under him or her. The first day is crucial because the employees will be sizing their boss up, noting every little thing he or she does or says. A certain opinion of their boss will be formed on the basis of their first encounter that will go a long way towards the success or failure of their relationship.

Obviously, every business is packed full of the data that we deal with in the study of the New Psychology. It has opinions and feelings that are either creative or destructive. Also, it is constantly creating opinions and feelings in the minds of its customers; and these opinions and feelings are either helpful or harmful. How to make them FAVOURABLE is the problem that must be solved.

CHAPTER 11

Making Use of Trends in Thought and Feeling

It is worthwhile giving a thought, now and then, to this question: "How can I keep in touch with things in this changing world?" It is certainly important to keep one's knowledge of events up-to-date. No one is so powerful or independent that they can safely afford to ignore what their contemporaries are doing and thinking.

We all know that young people can learn a good deal from older folk. But one fact that is often forgotten is that old people must tune in to the present by learning from the young.

We believe that intelligent people should think for themselves - that they should live their own lives. So they should, but that does not mean that they should ignore the trend of things going on around them. They may not agree with them, but they should certainly take note of them because they are not likely to make wise decisions unless they are aware of them.

Every nation experiences change. No nation stays still. If they do, they will soon be in trouble. Governments come and go. So do policies. Nothing in this world is permanent. There are always movements in some direction. This is what we call trends.

There are major and minor trends. There has never been an instant yet, of all nations pulling together in one direction. But among certain groupings of nations, distinct trends towards closer cooperation with each other can be noticed.

There are countries in Europe that have come together to form groups. The same goes for countries in South-East Asia, Central and South America. There are international trade organizations and currency agreements. All these are major trends in world affairs.

Minor trends may be noticed in the changes within specific countries, or in their various states, cities or towns. For instance, a state or city may be growing in a certain manner or direction. A speculator who watches these trends closely will take advantage of them by investing his money in a way that will pay big dividends in the future.

Then there are the speculators who keep a sharp eye on investment trends on the stock or commodities markets. There is always a general movement of prices either upward or downward - above or below the line of values. Price movements are controlled by many factors besides value - by many psychological influences. The person who buys or sells wisely knows this.

A trend of prices upwards quite often develops into a boom, followed by a depression or, if the depression worsens, a crash. This has been experienced more often in the United States, which is not a country of moderation. And if the United States, such a powerful country with such a massive economy, is hard hit, the rest of the world is bound to feel the effects of such an economic downturn.

Sometimes a trend becomes almost a mania. Entire nations stampede in a certain direction. One such case was during the Crusades, which lasted almost two centuries, from 1096 to 1291. The motive was, of course, religious. The motive is also frequently one of conquest or revenge, which invariably ends in nations going to war. At such times, the nation that acts irrationally and intolerantly is usually the aggressor. All civility and fair play then disappears and anyone who dares to defy the aggressors is liable to end up in prison or even be executed. A nation bent on destruction is often as blind and ruthless as a herd of stampeding elephants.

Stock exchange and commodity brokers also make it their business to study trends in the price of shares and commodities to help their clients make money on their investments. Experienced brokers can often predict which way the markets will swing. They develop a sixth sense in this respect. They study the signs of the times, and their aim is to acquire the ability to predict, almost with certainty, what will happen in the near future. They know when to buy, when to sell and when to hedge. Some business people are good at it too. But there is always the temptation to use "insider" or confidential information to manipulate share prices illegally for personal gain. This is called insider trading, and anyone caught dabbling in it can get into serious trouble with the law.

Foresight can also be acquired and applied when purchasing things. This can be done by studying mass or national movements - in a word, trends. Professional buyers are compelled to study these national movements. If they fail to do so, they are likely to over-buy or to make unwise selections.

Merchants can no longer ignore the trends in fashion either. They must do all they can to beat their many competitors by predicting what colours and designs are more likely to catch the eye of men and women in the near future. Fashions are transient. A new style springs up, commands top prices, becomes very popular, is reproduced at lower prices and dies out. All, perhaps, within a brief season. There are people whose business it is to create or foresee up-coming fashions. And their success depends on how well they study the trends.

Those who make a study of trends must take note of new highly profitable industries and of the old ones that are dying out. They must keep an eye on the laboratories that are discovering new synthetic products. No one today dare set a limit on what a chemist can or cannot do.

At any moment a new synthetic textile or food may make its appearance and provide opportunities to accumulate new fortunes. In 1935, for instance, the humble soya bean was imported into Britain for the first time in large quantities. For millions of people in the Third World, it has already become the source of a cheap, nourishing and palatable food. Today, it has been developed into a Textured Vegetable Protein (TVP), increasingly eaten as a protein substitute by vegetarians in the west and often added to meat products like luncheon meat, sausages and burgers.

It is possible to shape trends and, now and then, to create them. This can be done by advertising and propaganda. People can be taught new buying habits. The slogan "Say it with Flowers" certainly boosted sales at florists. Again and again, mass movements have been created by effective and persistent advertising.

If any firm is not large enough to create or shape a trend, it can at least do the second-best thing - it can study the latest trends and put itself in touch with them. No national movement or tendency can be ignored. If people can acquire even a little foresight to predict trends correctly, that knowledge can be turned to profitable use.

CHAPTER 12

Loyalty to the Truth

In order to make the best possible use of our mental powers, we must make it a rule to do what we can to distinguish between what is true and what is false. We must consciously develop a strong desire to seek out the Truth.

Quite a bit of what most of us believe is simply not true. There is no mental sieve in our minds to keep out what is false and to let through what is true. But when people are sincerely devoted to the truth, they will reject opinions that have no basis in fact.

In building structures of thought, we must be careful to use good materials. If we build with lies, we are only jerry-builders. Our structures will collapse. This is where many scholastic psychologists went wrong. They accepted the prevailing superstitions and opinions of their day. They lacked the devotion to seek out the truth that all scientists possess. They built their structures of thought with defective materials.

Truth is always the most useful asset in a person's life. This fact has become more evident in the business world today. When people's minds are cluttered up with all sorts of opinions and ideas they usually find it difficult to arrive at the right answers to practical problems.

Most people are inclined to accept the beliefs that prevail in the country in which they live. They have few ideas of their own. Their minds are muddled up with opinions and ideas put there by other people. This is only too true in countries run by dictators. Only a small percentage of people in any country are truly independent thinkers.

Every nation has a "dossier" containing all sorts of beliefs in connection with human life and its activities, and this is passed on from one generation to another. In progressive countries, these "dossiers" change as new beliefs are adopted. But these beliefs are not necessarily true - that is the point to remember.

Most people, including children, are inclined to hold fast to old beliefs. Many of these old tales are untrue. Some are brutal. But they have been overlaid with sentiment. The French Emperor Napoleon Bonaparte once said that "history is a fable agreed upon". And those of us who have seen history in the making would be inclined to agree. Most of the old tales have been embellished with half-truths and fiction over the years to become almost unrecognizable.

Most people, therefore, are not 100 per cent devoted to seeking out the truth because their loyalty lies with the "dossiers" of beliefs that have been handed down to them. Consequently, they are prejudiced against whatever is new or different. Many people who consider themselves practical and hard-headed, allow prejudices to cloud their thinking and decisions. They build their thought structures with defective materials. There are many prejudices even in the business world. None of us are quite as rational as we think we are. Often our decisions are influenced by prejudice which dies hard. There is, for instance, a silly prejudice against owning opals - one of the most beautiful of precious stones. Many people think they are unlucky. On the other hand, it would be just as foolish to consider them a "lucky" stone.

In spite of all the advances we have made, there are still three harmful prejudices in the business world. They are:

1. The prejudice against appointing young people to more senior posts.

Some societies still assume that seniority means superiority. When artists draw pictures of people who are supposed to represent wisdom, they usually depict them as old people with long grey hair, with wrinkles and bushy eyebrows. Wisdom, of course, is not the preserve of the elderly only. This is only a myth which the old keep on telling the young.

In almost every company there are young people who are fitted for higher positions. They are held down simply because they are young and lack experience even if they have the paper qualifications. If they don't have the qualifications, then there are two strikes against them - no papers as well as insufficient experience. In a well organized company, the leadership should be more or less shared equally by the older and younger people. Each has useful qualities to contribute.

2. The prejudice against having women in higher positions.

There is still the delusion that leadership is a man's job. Comparatively few women sit on our boards of directors. It would indeed be funny to see an all-male company, including its board of directors, running an organization that manufactures and sells women's under-garments.

Women are the money-power. They buy between 70 to 80 per cent of the goods. This indicates that women should be given a larger share in the management of our companies. The masculine brain is not the standard brain. That is a delusion that we must get rid of. There is no sex in brains.

3.   The prejudice against having the so-called "uneducated" in higher positions.

Many companies hold back competent people merely because of race, looks or accent or because they don't speak very well, don't have an honours degree or didn't graduate from one of the "elite" higher institutes of learning. It is far better to employ someone who does a job well and then says simply: "I've done it," than to have someone with a string of titles after his name who botches up the job and then says in perfect English: "As a matter of fact, I found the difficulties quite insurmountable."

We still consider a drawing-room education as a big plus in favour of someone who applies for a good position in the business world. We prefer a small imperfectly cut diamond to a large, uncut one. We allow this prejudice to upset our sense of real values.

As we grow older, we find it harder to get rid of old prejudices and obsolete opinions. We dislike having to admit that we have changed our minds. This puts us out of touch with a changing world. It also hurts us mentally and morally. The pinnacle of good character and breeding cannot be attained without a deep desire to always seek out the truth.

CHAPTER 13

The Value of Novel-Reading

One of the prejudices or mistaken beliefs to which I referred in a previous chapter is that busy, purposeful people should not waste their time reading novels. And as this is a practical book on the New Psychology, I am compelled to say that one of the best ways to acquire a wide knowledge of psychology is to read good novels.

Having been an avid reader of novels all my life, I think it only fair that I should, in one of my books, express my feeling of gratitude to novelists. The effect of their books on the broadening of the mind and the development of one's sympathies is usually undervalued. It is entirely ignored by many people.

A novel enables us to get to know how others live. It puts us in touch with classes of people whom we may never meet in real life. It is a sort of substitute for personal experience. It enables us to sit in an armchair at home and get to know all about peoples and places without leaving the front door. It lifts us out of the little circles in which we live, and broadens our minds. Surely, all this makes it worthwhile to cultivate the habit of reading novels.

Books are broadly divided into fiction, non-fiction or factual and autobiographical. When they are factual or autobiographical, they deal with the lives and feelings of real people and are not only interesting but educational. Very often, books on fiction are based on factual events, in which case the characters in the novel are given fictitious names, and in some cases, the locations are as well.

Like everything else, a lot of trash can also be found in novels. So it is very important to pay close attention to the selection of reading material. Novel-reading can do much to shape your thinking and temperament. It can do much to curb our temperamental faults or add fuel to them. Often, we are able to see a reflection of ourselves as others see us.

Good novels also help to relax a tired or overworked mind. I have usually found that people in business who say they have "no time" to read novels are those who really need them most. It does not pay to have one's mind always tense and concentrated on work. The mind needs some kind of diversion now and then. For this reason, if for no other, a busy person should make a habit of reading novels.

Curling up with a well-written novel is almost as good as talking to someone. Even better, if that someone is not much of a conversationalist. People get to know the characters in the book intimately. They feel they know all there is to know about them - their joys, sorrows and adventures.

I am particularly fond of detective stories. I must say that they are, in my opinion, very useful as well as interesting to people in business. Detective mysteries confront the reader with problems of detection. There are clues to unravel in order to solve the crimes and it is the detective's business to search for those clues. Consequently, such stories enliven the brain. They turn the readers into armchair detectives.

Likewise, it is the job of people in business to look for clues to boost profits. The art of observation and deduction, described in detective stories, is of tremendous value in the business world. Bosses are not looking for criminals but for clues to build up their business, and reading such stories helps them to sharpen their wits.

As to reading love stories - why not? The hard people who do not read them never know what they lose. At one time people believed in the delusion that there is no sentiment in business. All that is past history.

Somehow, no catalogue of influences that have moulded English life is complete without mentioning the novels of Charles Dickens. It is certain that his books had a greater effect upon the English people than the legislation of his day. Dickens ripened the British people - mellowed them - gave them a wider range of sympathies.

They admire Shakespeare but they love Dickens. Shakespeare saw no value in the lives of the poor and the down-trodden. His heroes and heroines lived in castles. Dickens, however, was the first English author to point out to his people a beauty and nobility in the lives of simple folk. The fact that fair play is one of the most universal of British virtues is owed, in no small measure, to the writings of Dickens.

The character and opinions of most civilized nations have been shaped to a large extent by novels. Ask anyone: "What book, in your opinion, has done most to mould the character of the people in your country?" and he is most likely to give you not only the name of the book, but also the author's name. If he is a Frenchman, he might say "The Three Musketeers" by Alexander Dumas or "The Hunchback of Nortre Dame" by Victor Hugo. If he is an American, he might plum for John Steinbeck's "Grapes of Wrath", or simply say "Don Quixote" if he is a Spaniard, and so on.

As you can see, it is a mistake for busy, purposeful people to be contemptuous of that class of literature that, I consider, is wrongly labelled as "fiction." Never before has there been as many good novels in bookstores as there are today. And I think these people should make it a point to read them. They should even read the so-called "best sellers" to find out what makes those novels so interesting to the tens of thousands of readers. In order to get to know more about the people of our day, we must know what kind of books they are reading.

CHAPTER 14

The Value of Travel

This subject, like novel-reading, may not be found in most books on psychology, but most people will admit that travel has a formative influence on the mind and character. Those who have lived abroad for some time certainly broaden their outlook of life over those who choose to stay at home. What can the villager who spends his whole life in his village know about the world outside? People who have never travelled outside their home towns tend to take a very narrow view of things and are highly suspicious of strangers or visitors.

Travel also has some curative effect on people with emotional and even physical problems. Doctors sometimes suggest a change of scenery for some people with such problems. New surroundings, new faces, customs and the change of climate and food seem to have some beneficial therapeutic effect on them. It encourages them to look outward - to reach out to people instead of being overly concerned with their personal problems. This is especially so after a bereavement. Travel and time are the two best healers when the mind is overwhelmed by grief.

Seeing new places and meeting new people are also tremendous stimulants when people find themselves in a rut - when the mind becomes stale and refuses to be creative. It may be due to monotony of their jobs - the same old routine and the same old faces day in and day out. The best way to "revive" their jaded brains is to spend some time travelling, if they can afford it. If they can't then they will have to be content with taking long walks or bus or train rides to neighbouring counties or states.

Heads of business organizations have always found it wise to travel now and then to some quiet place to get an overview of their business affairs without being bothered by the monotony of details and routine work. Quite a few businesses slow down because the top people persist in holding fast to small jobs instead of delegating them to their subordinates. When people are in foreign countries, they are more likely to be receptive to new ideas and notice new methods. They are always more observant. A new environment opens their minds and their eyes.

Travel can and does help people in business cultivate contacts and observe local market conditions at first hand. This applies especially to manufacturers. People who are connected with the selling side of their organizations should also travel extensively. Foreign sales cannot be increased by mail order alone. No one can possibly know how business in a foreign country operates, what its people or customs are like, unless he has spent some time in it.

There can be no doubt that travel does more to promote international trade and goodwill than any other thing. It broadens people's minds and makes them more tolerant. And it enables them to seize business opportunities that they would not otherwise notice if they sat glued to their chairs in their offices.

Europe was roused out of the lethargy of the Dark Ages by travel, first of all by the Crusades, and then by the exploits of those adventurous navigators. The psychological effect of the voyages of Christopher Columbus has never been, and will probably never be, fully described by any writer. In 1492 there was a change in the mentality of the people of Europe. Columbus did vastly more than discover America. He helped Europeans to discover their adventurous spirit.

The golden age of Queen Elizabeth the First was not made golden by the people who stayed at home. It was made glorious by those courageous navigators - most of all by Sir Francis Drake. The exploits of the English sailors gave the English people an ambition that made them irresistible. When they took to the sea, the foundations of the British Empire were laid. But what has been accomplished since then in sea travel - the huge oil tankers, ocean-going luxury liners and the nuclear-powered aircraft carriers and submarines - would startle and amaze the maritime nations of the Elizabethan era.

There are now trains in Japan, France and the United States that travel faster than some of the aircraft used in World War II. Today's fighter aircraft routinely fly faster then the speed of sound. What about the sleek Anglo-French Concorde - the luxury airliner that lets you have breakfast in London and dinner in Singapore the same day - some 12,000 kilometres apart. The most distinctive developments in our day have been in the field of travel.

We do not need a prophet to foresee the eventual psychological effects of increased travel. In spite of temporary waves of nationalism now and then, nations are learning to get to know one another better and increase cooperation. The jerry-built League of Nations has made way for the United Nations, permanently sited in New York City. Communications today, both audio and visual, is merely a matter of pushing buttons - by telephone, by computer, by telex, fax and television. The world has suddenly become very small indeed. Certainly, people should now see as much of it as they can while they are still alive.

CHAPTER 15

Emotional Influences

The English philosopher Herbert Spencer once said that "the brain is half feeling". He may not have been the first person to make this observation, but it influenced other thinkers to pay more attention to the emotional influences that affect the mental activities of human beings.

These emotional influences may strengthen or weaken people. The main point to remember is that the stronger they are, the more will-power is needed to control them. No feeling or emotion should ever be allowed to dominate or rule the brain. The thinking or reasoning portion of the brain must do it. That should be the rule if we are to keep our sanity.

Emotion is like a swift river. It may be channelled to be useful. It may turn wheels and create electricity. Or it may be destructive when it breaks its barriers, creating havoc.

Emotion can also give people a wonderful sense of power. It may win for them the love and loyalty of others or make them leaders. But unless they can control it effectively, it could easily wreck them and others with them. It could destroy their ability to think reasonably or rationally. People must learn to be masters of their emotions. They must develop self-control. Without it, they could become destructive, ready to inflict suffering and humiliation at the slightest provocation.

They must learn to recognize their weak points and develop their will-power to overcome such weaknesses. They must never allow emotion to triumph in place of reason, and to do this their minds must be constantly disciplined.

Those, for instance, who are habitually angry over trifles, become ineffective thinkers. Their wrath explodes like a car's exhaust pipe. It constantly upsets the train of their thoughts, and destroys their influence on their associates. They become confused and disorientated. Worst of all, they become irrational. Anger is a power that should be used only on very special occasions. It should be regarded as a reserve power. People who have no latent anger are likely to be pushed around in this jostling world. There are times when anger is a valuable asset. But there is no doubt that the safest and best rule is to use it as sparingly as possible.

When emotions are allowed to run riot, the brain is in turmoil. They cloud the brain and prevent clear thinking. Logic, common sense and even self-interest are tossed aside. In a fit of rage, people may beat up their wives, drive their children out of their homes or worse still, even commit murder.

The process of thought is like a conference being staged in a person's mind. If this conference is disturbed by intrusive emotions, the person cannot think clearly or concentrate on the thought process. If one of the stronger feelings or emotions - anger, jealously or grief - gets out of control, the brain becomes chaotic and the result could mean violence.

What takes place in the brain then is what often takes place at rowdy political meetings. Hecklers try their best to prevent the speaker from speaking. They shout, scream, sing and even hurl objects at the speaker in a bid to drown out his voice. This sort of rowdyism takes place because reason, logic and common sense are replaced by emotions of anger and hatred. It is precisely in situations like this that people may resort to the kind of violence they may regret for the rest of their lives.

It is a fact that people who habitually stimulate their baser feelings will eventually lose their ability to think rationally. They lose their self-control, their self-respect and everything else that makes for decent living.

I know of a tragic story in which a detective accidentally discovered that his great-grandfather was a hangman. Admittedly, it was not a very nice thing to discover about one's ancestry, but not something any level-headed person would go off the deep end over. However, the detective apparently was not a level-headed person. Instead of talking to someone close about it - getting it off his chest and then forgetting about it - he began to brood. He became moody, stopped seeing his friends and almost became a hermit. The final blow came when he lost his job. To his twisted mind, it was like an indictment against him - telling him that there was no more use for him because of his great-grandfather. So he went out and killed a person - a total stranger. Such things do happen when someone loses the power to think rationally.

Tragic things also happen in business because of emotional influences. So it is important to remember that the twin stabilizers of the mind - logic and common sense - must always prevail in a clash with one's baser emotions. The best way to ensure this is to develop one's will-power and self-control.

CHAPTER 16

Acquiring a Helpful Temperament

All people are temperamental - each one in a different manner. The differences in temperament can be noticed in little
children. One may be quiet and affectionate, while another
may be sociable and gay. A mother with five or six children
will have to deal effectively with five or six different temperaments.

Most people stand a good chance of retaining their inherited
temperaments throughout their lives, not necessarily for the
worse. What I would like to point out is that people can do
something to change the bad or defective aspects of their
temperament.

During a family quarrel or fight with friends, people might say:
"Well, that is the disposition I was born with. I can't help it."
They place the blame on heredity. But they are consciously or
unconsciously deceiving themselves. People have both inherited and acquired characteristics. It has been found that it
is possible for people to change their characteristics. This has
been done time and again by those with strong wills.

A genius may be forgiven for being temperamental. When
people have proved that they are original and creative, when
they have achieved distinction in whatever field they apply
themselves to, they have earned the right to certain liberties
that cannot be extended to everyone. We are ready to forgive
them their oddities and even their rudeness. But even a genius
should not be allowed to say or do everything he pleases.

The artistic temperament - we come across it now and then in the business world - is in many instances only an excuse for a disagreeable disposition and an over-developed self-conceit, as all those in the entertainment business know very well. It is taken as a licence to be rude to other people - as a justification for oddities and excesses in behaviour.

Quite often, a little success goes to people's heads and helps them to develop their faults in temperament. Sales managers are aware that there are some successful sales people who are as hard to manage as prima donnas. They place themselves on a pedestal and forget that they should set a good example to their colleagues who are less successful.

There are difficult people to get on with in every company, factory or organization. They are touchy - quick to take offence. Some of them are so thin-skinned that they should wear a sign saying: "Beware! I am fragile." They go out of their way to make a nuisance of themselves over trifling things.

It is a fact that temperamental people are self-centered, childish and difficult to please. They expect people to be considerate but are not considerate themselves. They create a tense atmosphere wherever they are that is not conducive to anything, especially good work.

Daily-paid workers are inclined to be temperamental, possibly because they lack, they believe, the job security of monthly, fortnightly or weekly-paid workers. They have been known to stir up trouble among their colleagues and those who oversee them.

There is an old story of a farmer who had three cows. One gave three litres a day of high quality milk. The second gave six litres a day of low quality milk. The third gave six litres a day of high quality milk, but she kicked the pail over once a week. As you can see, not one of the three was a first-class cow. One had a small output of high quality. The second had a big output of low quality. And the third had a big output of high quality, but she had a bad disposition and tipped over one-seventh of her milk.

There are many workers who are like these three cows. Some who have skill lack energy. Some who have energy lack skill. And some who have both skill and energy are as hard to manage as film stars. Almost every employer has found this to be true. The best worker - the one who is likely to be promoted - is the one who has skill, energy and a good disposition. He is sure to attract the attention and win the goodwill of those who are in authority over him.

In every organisation, temperamental defects create friction. They prevent the smooth-running efficiency that is essential for the best results. Many people - sometimes very able ones - lose their positions or businesses because of defects in disposition that might have been overcome. We have all known of such instances. People who constantly create friction cause serious losses to the business they are in.

So, it goes without saying that those who inherit trouble-making dispositions should endeavour to be more stoical - to be less easily upset. They can school themselves to give their undivided attention to everything that deserves to be done and ignore the unpleasant trifles. It is quite possible to acquire a poise of mind that will enable them to move more evenly and pleasantly through their work and recreation.

Perhaps the most effective cure for temperamental defects is to think more of the opinions and feelings of others. People can teach themselves to be considerate and set for themselves a higher standard of behaviour. They can modify the temperament they inherited and make it much more helpful in the achievement of both success and happiness, if only they will learn to think more of others than of themselves.

CHAPTER 17

The Truth About Worrying

People who are chronic worriers cannot think effectively. Worry is as common to the psyche as food is to the body. Some people talk about getting rid of it. It cannot be done. You can no more get rid of it than stop yourself from breathing. But there are some preventable worries and there are some that are not worth bothering about because nothing can be done about them. Anyway, no one need be a slave to worry or let it assume such unreasonable proportions that it gets completely out of hand.

It is true that there are some people who do not seem to know what worry means. They appear to be carefree and seldom live lives that are of any use to the world.

As a rule, such people are drifters and are usually idle and parasitical. They are not purposeful. Certainly, they cannot be held up as a class of people to be admired or worthy of imitation. But they do worry - at least to the extent of wondering where their next meal is coming from or where they are going to sleep for the night.

People who work for a living cannot stop themselves from worrying now and then. But not all worrying is harmful. There have been critical moments in the lives of great men and women that caused them to worry, no matter how completely they controlled their emotions in their minds. The point to note and remember is that their worrying was not harmful, if it led them to study the CAUSE of the worry and take action.

Business people OUGHT to worry if their business is in a rut, with profits decreasing, competitors leaving them behind, poor economic outlook and so on. It becomes very evident that worry will be far more useful to such people than complacency.

The fact is that worry may be a help, not a hindrance, in business life, if people ask themselves this question: "What can be done?" Those who are competent and well-adjusted do not allow their worries to discourage them. They accept them as a matter of course and do their best to grapple with the causes behind them.

Often, worries are caused by something that is beyond anyone's power to deal with. They may stem from government actions, by what we call an "act of God", or by people over whom we have no control. In such cases, worry is not only unhelpful but useless, and people should do their best to forget it. They would be on target if they worry over their own mistakes or about anything else that they can control, but not over things they cannot change.

French statesman Georges Clemenceau is reported to have told English statesman Lloyd George: "Abuse has never kept me awake for an hour, but I have often been kept awake when I felt that I had made a fool of myself." And Lloyd George is reported to have replied: "I, too, never mind being abused, but if I feel that I have made a fool of myself I could kick myself out of bed." In other words, people should worry about only what is in their own power to change, and should then take action to improve it.

Those who say we should not worry at all - that all worry is preventable - are pure theorists. That is, in my opinion, a foolish and impossible doctrine. As far as I know, there is nothing in any book or in my own experience to convince me of any useful formula to stop worrying.

Worry is often caused by our love for others. A mother worries when her child is sick. A father worries when his only son is living a life of dissipation. Who would not worry if his doctor said to him: "You have an incurable disease"?

There are some types of worries which cannot be cured. All that we can do is accept what we cannot change and make the best of it. But no worry should be put in this category until the reason for it has been carefully studied and all possible solutions attempted. It should be pointed out that acceptance or resignation becomes a fault, not a virtue, if we put up with troubles that a strong, determined effort will overcome.

Nothing, of course, can be said in favour of the chronic worrier who seems to be always looking for something to fret about. Such people make life unpleasant both at home and at work. Their worries are usually futile. They have acquired a distasteful habit that is of no use to anyone, especially to themselves.

Some people, especially in managerial positions, are always angry. They are most unpleasant to work with. An old man I knew read every line in the newspaper in the hope of finding something to grumble about. Some people feel this sort of thing makes them appear superior in some way or other.

A great deal of friction is created by this bad habit of looking out for something to be annoyed at, or unhappy about. The way to go through life more smoothly and effectively is to give praise when it is due and to make useful suggestions when correction is needed.

Generally, it is better to cultivate the habit of looking on the bright side than to plague people into apathy by perpetual fault-finding. When people find they can no longer please their bosses, no matter what they say or do, you may be sure that they will soon stop trying to do so.

The best cure for preventable worries is creative thinking. When worry becomes a spur to action, we can include it among our mental assets. Success depends mainly on the ability to face obstacles and unpleasant facts. In short, worry can be either a deadly germ or the seed from which success sprouts.

CHAPTER 18

Overcoming Fear

Fear, like worry, interferes with effective thinking. I will not go so far as to say that it clouds CLEAR thinking, but it is certainly true to say that it weakens the will-power and consequently prevents action from being taken. Fear has a paralysing effect upon the will.

Very often, fear is the underlying reason behind the chronic worrier. Sometimes, people know what they should do to rid themselves of fear but do nothing because they are afraid to take the plunge. They are held back by fear - a case of fear feeding on fear. It may take someone with a strong personality to help them muster enough courage to take action.

People who do nothing to control or fight their fears will eventually develop a mentality so unreasonably governed by fear that it could impel them to do drastic or foolish things. Panic-stricken people are always apt to say or do silly, often dangerous, things. When in such a situation these people should do nothing at all until they regain a measure of self-confidence.

Fear destroys happiness. No one pays more for money then the one who steals it. Even if his theft is not discovered, a thief is still punished because his peace of mind has been destroyed. He is always apprehensive. Even in his sleep he is likely to dream of being found out. Many guilty people have been goaded by fears to such an extent that they are driven to end it all by taking their own lives.

The business world is full of fears. The news served up by newspapers every day is mostly bad. From the journalist's point of view, a minor item of bad news is more interesting and sells better than a major item of good news. This has become a difficult and dangerous world for timid people to live in.

In order to succeed, business people must be like ocean liners - they must make their way in spite of the waves, winds, storms and fogs. And like ships that make money only when they are moving, people must be on the move to get on. No matter what the dangers are, there is always something that can be done. We must accept danger as one of the inescapable conditions of life. But one of the most cheering thoughts about danger is - most of the things that we are afraid of usually do not happen.

The people who should remember this most are those in sales - especially those who are selling their products on the move. Naturally they will be somewhat apprehensive about making a good impression on customers and being able to satisfy certain standards set by their respective companies. The biggest fear of inexperienced salesmen is being brushed off rudely. They have to literally force themselves to go into some places. Most of them, however, will discover after a while that all their apprehensions were groundless - no dogs bit them, no one threw them out or threw things at them.

People in managerial positions should confront their fears instead of giving in to them. They should try to get to the root cause of their fears and do all they can to master them. And they should never, under any circumstances, instil fear in their subordinates as a managerial weapon. It is a great mistake for bosses to try to create fear in the minds of those working under them.

Fear decreases efficiency in any business organization. It destroys loyalty, and lowers both productivity and quality of work. People who are constantly thinking of their own security are not likely to work well. An employer who can motivate his workers is likely to get three times as much work out of them as one who pushes them with threats.

It was common practice in the early days of business to use rigid, disciplinary army methods to drive workers. The single-minded belief then was that people had to be goaded - made to work - by threats and various penalties.

No one then thought of such things as winning the goodwill of workers, so that they would need less and less supervision. Workers then were supposed to be driven like cattle. Only one thing mattered above all else - getting work out of them. The aim today is to motivate employees to give of their best with the aid of all sorts of incentives and training programmes.

Of course, there will always be a few bosses around who will continue to shout, swear and threaten, and some who even wish they could carry whips. By and large, however, fear has been abolished in the workplace. It has taken courage and the far-sightedness of some people to bring this about. Civilization, after all, has not destroyed courage - one of the foundation stones in the building of character.

One of the best tests of a person's character is his attitude to danger. Courage is both inherited and acquired. Many timid people have overcome their fears. I have found that the best formula for acquiring courage is a very simple one - do, or attempt to do, something that has an element of danger in it every day. If people will do this, they will eventually conquer the weaker side of their nature and prepare themselves to tackle greater dangers and bigger challenges.

CHAPTER 19

Home Life

Home life is seldom a topic in any book on metaphysical psychology. The New Psychology, however, certainly cannot ignore its powerful influence, for better or worse, on people who are determined to develop a career.

The home is a most important factor. Some people draw immense energy and fortitude from their home life, while, for others, it has the opposite effect.

Those with happy home lives possess a most valuable asset. It is priceless and does more than anything else to create a stable, well-balanced mental outlook. It has a recuperative influence on people with heavy responsibilities, and gives them the courage and fortitude to face whatever trials and hardships that life brings.

Home is man's emotional headquarters. Here, people reach the heights of joy and, perhaps, the depths of sorrow. No one should take the home lightly, as though it is only a place to eat and sleep in. Whether it helps or hinders, a home remains the centre of the lives of all living in it.

To have a happy, successful home life requires a technique of its own. Many of the world's so-called wisest men and women know little or nothing about home life because they are too busy with other things to bother much about it. The best authority to expound on how to make the best of home life is, without doubt, a couple who have been happily married for half a century or more.

The best thing that can happen to any young person in business is picking the right marriage partner. So often we read or hear about marriage break-ups, leaving both partners confused and their children, if any, even more confused. When people in business are cheered on and helped by their partners in life, you can be almost 100 per cent sure that whatever they undertake to do will be a success.

To keep a husband in the right humour to make the most of himself and his business - that is a large part of the technique of wifehood. Even if she does not work, a good wife earns her full share of the family fortune - not that this should be the only reason for a woman to be a good wife. Similarly, it is the duty of husbands to help their wives in every way possible to fulfil their needs and goals.

There are many homes where communication has been reduced to just one or two syllable words. It is worse still in some homes where speech does not exist, not even between spouses and their children. Home life like this does nothing to help people lead well-balanced lives or encourage them to interact meaningfully with others outside their homes.

There is nothing that money can buy or that fame can bring that can take the place of a happy home. In some homes, children say: "Quiet! Here comes Father." In other homes they might say: "Hooray! Here comes Dad." There is a world of difference between these two greetings. It is when some children begin to feel far more at home in other people's houses that their parents should sit up and begin to reassess their relationship with them.

It is one of the common tragedies of life that many people who set out to make happy homes - to give their families the best that money can buy - eventually become so absorbed in their business that they shut themselves off from their loved ones completely.

Inevitably, either the wife or the husband or both, if the wife is a career woman, will find themselves neglected and proceed to build up interests of their own elsewhere. They are compelled to do this in self-defence for the sake of their own happiness. They will inevitably seek outside companionship, usually with office colleagues. So, the stage of alienation has been set, followed, perhaps, by quarrels and eventually divorce proceedings. And there goes one more broken home.

People should do their best to develop both sides of their nature - the working or head-power as well as the home or heart-power. A home should not be a mere bedroom nor an evening office. The cares of the day should be left outside the front door. It should be a place of relaxation - a place that draws out all a man's or a woman's social qualities and affection. It should be a peaceful and cheerful refuge from the cares of working life.

People should strive for success and happiness in life. Business-builders must be home-makers as well if they want to reap the full reward of their labours.

CHAPTER 20

The Psychological Effect of Humour

It is said of a famous general that he laughed only once in his life - when he heard of the death of his mother-in-law. Surely such a grim character could not have brought much joy to the people in his life.

No doubt the exalted position of an army general seems to call for a pose of unsmiling severity. Some jobs may require dignity above all else, but the point I want to make in this final chapter is that this "lofty" attitude should have no place in the business world. Unfortunately, it does. And never in my long life have I seen the slightest necessity for the tremendous amount of dignity and severity that does exist among many people in business.

The origin of this blight of dignity, that does so much to make trade and industry ridiculous, has evidently been handed down from the Age of Feudalism to the Industrial Age. The first business organizations of the Industrial Age were patterned on the rather rigid structures of the Church's priesthood and the feudal armies. And many of the absurd poses and pomposities of militarism were carried into business life.

This goes far to explain the solemnity of some board meetings and business conferences. It explains the use of a formal semi-legal jargon in the writing of business letters. It explains the aloofness and almost Papal infallibility of many bosses who sit secluded and protected in their offices, like high and mighty gods and goddesses.

All this solemnity and sanctity of authority is, I venture to say, purely traditional. We now realize that it has its comic side. A business conference is not a ritualistic ceremony. There is no good reason why there should be any element of worship or servility in any business group.

What does business mean? It means serving people. It means working with people and for people. It calls for the development of all the social qualities. It compels us to think of winning the goodwill of others. It demands sociability and one of the elements of sociability is HUMOUR. Many of the ablest people in business have now discovered that friendliness and humour are factors in good management and in business-building. They know that laughter relaxes and relieves the mind, prevents friction and gains the favourable attention of the public.

We now realize the immense psychological value of humour in every aspect of life. We also know that all that solemnity and false dignity is unprofitable as well as absurd. Most business organizations now publish in-house magazines packed with light human-interest stories and humour.

Despite writing for many serious, purposeful people, I would venture to say that one of the best profit-makers in the business world is FUN. Lots of people in business go through the day without even a smile. They become so serious that they probably do not even laugh at home. This could cost them more than they know. When people lose their sense of humour, they more likely than not lose money as well. Make no mistake about that.

Fun is a lubricant in business. It banishes worry. It helps people to relax, removes tension and prevents clashes and fatigue. It is the best promoter of enthusiasm which, in turn, has a magical effect on productivity.

I guarantee that anyone who makes a habit of cracking a joke or two with people on the way to the office every day will be in fine shape to start work. All of us enjoyed laughing when we were kids. We were all for fun. And I think we would all succeed more easily if we let ourselves be more like kids at heart.

To say that the most dignified people are also the wisest is a myth. It is also out of traditional belief that some artists represent Wisdom as a grim-looking, bearded dignitary. The belief that wisdom comes with age is also a myth.

I believe no country, except the United States, has ever erected a statue to a comedian. It would be wise of us to learn to appreciate comedy more. It is one of the good signs of the times that more people are flocking to see comedians. I believe such people will benefit from them far more than they realize. People in business are now aware that a little humour and sociability is useful in introducing any new policy or launching any project. If introduced with too much solemnity, they are likely to create fear and opposition.

Every able speaker knows the effectiveness of a joke. It unifies an audience and makes the listeners receptive. A story is told of an English diplomat who was sent to represent his country at an international conference. There were delegates from 12 other nations. A rather delicate subject was on the agenda to be discussed. All the delegates, except the Englishman, were tense and suspicious. He strode into the conference with a big smile, sat down and from his pocket produced an interesting new mechanical toy he bought for his son. He wound the toy up, put it on the table and in no time the other delegates were laughing. The tension disappeared, the conference began pleasantly and soon a unanimous decision was reached. That little incident represents what I mean by the psychology of humour.

Older people are inclined to be somewhat alarmed at the many types of new entertainment being provided for the amusement of people. They do not need to be worried. The popularity of these entertainments is not a sign of decadence. Light hearts do not mean light brains. The longer I live, the more I am inclined to say a good word for frivolity. Is it not true that during Christmas and other festive seasons, department stores and other places are turned into fun arcades? Do they not become frivolous? Has this not been found to be a profitable policy? And would it not be a good idea to allow this kind of spirit to prevail all year round?

The truth is that life is too serious to take it too seriously. Surely it is wise for us, then, to make life as least a tragedy as possible - to relieve it with humour - to add a bit to its glory and its joy.

Our lives last only a short time on this tiny planet we call Earth. We are comic when we strut. We are absurd when we pose as super people or super nations. We should be glad to be alive while we work, play, think, laugh and love. Whoever does this, and does it well, will have made good use of his life.

BRASH BOOKS BOOK CLUB
GRAHAM BRASH (PTE) LTD
HEAD OFFICE, SALES & WAREHOUSE
32 GUL DRIVE, SINGAPORE 2262.
TEL: 8611336, 8620437
TELEX: RS 23718 FEENIX GB
FAX: 65-8614815

We hope that you have enjoyed reading this book by **Graham Brash**. It is one in a list of over 600 publications covering a wide range of subject areas. To find out more about related titles, you can join our book club today.

BRASH BOOKS is a specialised book club which selects publications for its members according to their reading interests. Membership is free and book information, special discounts and other benefits (invitations to book-signings, for example) are mailed to members regularly.

To join **BRASH BOOKS** , simply complete this form and either fax or mail it to the above address. Upon receipt, a free catalogue will be forwarded to you. Thank you for becoming a **BRASH BOOK** reader.

Name: ....   Tel/Fax: ....

Address: ....   Date of Birth : ....

....   Occupation: ....

....   Marital Status: ....

Area(s) of Interest:

(   ) Asian Interest   (   ) Others (please specify):

(   ) Asian Literature   1) ....

(   ) Mind, Body, Spirit   2) ....

(   ) Business/Management/   3) ....

     Self-Improvement   Languages:

(   ) Fiction – Adult   (   ) German

(   ) Fiction – Children   (   ) French

(   ) Education/Study   (   ) Others (please specify):

(   ) General Interest   ....